Mi

Of e

know you are the one
who uses these things
to get thru all you've
been thru. This book
made me think of you.
I'm so blessed to have
you as my best friend

Love you,
Always Cela

Secrets of EMOTIONAL HEALING

J. Donald Walters

Hardbound edition, 1995

ISBN 1-56589-044-2
10 9 8 7 6 5 4 3 2 1

Illustrations: Sarah Moffatt
Design: Crystal Clarity Design
Art Direction: Christine Schuppe

Printed in China

14618 Tyler Foote Road
Nevada City, CA 95959
1-800-424-1055

A Seed thought is offered for every day of the month. Begin a day at the appropriate date. Repeat the saying several times: first out loud, then softly, then in a whisper, and then only mentally. With each repetition, allow the words to become absorbed ever more deeply into your subconscious.

Thus, gradually, you will acquire a complete understanding of each day's thought. At this point, indeed, the truths set forth here will have become your own.

Keep the book open at the pertinent page throughout the day. Refer to it occasionally during moments of leisure. Relate the saying as often as possible to real situations in your life.

Then at night, before you go to bed, repeat the thought several times more. While falling asleep, carry the words into your subconscious, absorbing their positive influence into your whole being. Let it become thereby an integral part of your normal consciousness.

The secret of overcoming anger
is relinquishing personal desire,
by relating your emotions to a
broader arc of feeling: love for a
friend; or joy in inner freedom
from external circumstances; or
respect for the right of others
to make their own decisions, and
their own mistakes.

DAY ONE

The secret of overcoming anxiety is to do your best in the present, without attachment to the outcome, knowing that whatever is yours by right must come to you sooner or later, and that all else, even if acquired, will prove evanescent.

The secret of overcoming
depression is useful activity,
devoted selflessly
to helping others.

DAY THREE

The secret of overcoming depression is not to try reasoning your way out of the slump, but vigorously to raise your level of energy from the heart to the brain, then channeling it outward in creative activity, or in useful service to others.

DAY FOUR

The secret of overcoming depression is to affirm mentally, "I am not my moods, and I am not subject to the moods of others. I am ruler in my kingdom of thoughts and feelings!" In everything you do, strive to be a cause, not an effect.

DAY FIVE

The secret of overcoming discouragement is working to instill courage in others.

DAY SIX

The secret of overcoming discouragement is not to brood: Instead, act! Uplift your heart's feelings. Stand upright; inhale, and with the inhalation draw courage upward from your heart to your forehead; then exhale, and cast out of yourself all mental weakness and negativity.

DAY SEVEN

The secret of overcoming loneliness is to develop the company of inner "friends" — creative thoughts, high ideals, and noble aspirations. Visualize your mind as a nation, and its thought-population as happy, self-motivated citizens.

The secret of overcoming loneliness is to practice the presence of God, and share with Him every thought, every feeling, every action.

DAY NINE

The secret of overcoming unkind thoughts is to reflect that the person you hurt most, when you are uncharitable, is yourself; but that the principal recipient also of your blessings, when you are kind to others, is yourself.

DAY TEN

The secret of overcoming
hurt feelings is to expect
nothing of others;
thus, their words and
actions will always find
you inwardly at peace.

DAY ELEVEN

*The secret of overcoming
hurt feelings is
to direct your attention
outward, in giving of
yourself to others, instead
of dwelling self-centeredly on
your expectations of them.*

*The secret of overcoming
cynicism is to concentrate
on the needs of others, and not to
dwell on the thought
that life, or other people,
owe it to you to be different
from what they are.*

The secret of overcoming
bitterness is not
allowing yourself to feel
that you deserve more
from life than you are getting.
For life will always mete out
to you exactly what you
earn from it.

The secret of overcoming dependence on others is to reflect: Can a person gain anything from anyone that doesn't resonate with something he already possesses in himself? Live more from within. From that center, radiate your own special strength and courage to all.

DAY FIFTEEN

The secret of overcoming discontentment is to realize that conditions are always essentially neutral: Whether they please or displease depends on the attitudes we hold in our hearts. Practice, therefore, being ever happy in yourself.

DAY SIXTEEN

The secret of overcoming doubt is to concentrate on your reasons for gratitude to life, and not to focus on all those things which seem to you imperfect. Love other people. Love truth. ***Love!*** *Fill your heart with generous sentiments, and doubts will flee like shadows before the sunrise.*

The secret of overcoming mental dullness is to train yourself to say "**Yes!**" instantly, whenever your impulse is to grumble, or to cry, "No!" Welcome life in all its variety and challenges. Like the petals of a daisy, keep your heart open to life's experiences. Overcome within you the tendency to rejection and withdrawal.

DAY EIGHTEEN

The secret of
overcoming fearfulness
is to seek peace at that
calm center within, where
nothing can touch you: neither
fire, nor flood, nor loss of
any kind, — not even death.

DAY NINETEEN

The secret of overcoming feelings of guilt is to relinquish the past; for whatever has been done can't be undone. Resolve, instead, to do better from today onward — and ever better, until that "better" becomes the very best that is in you. View your mistakes as prods, merely, to ultimate victory.

DAY TWENTY

The secret of overcoming greed is contentment! harmonious feelings in the heart. Affirm mentally: "I am complete in myself. I am whole! I am free from all anxiety and need! Contentedly I accept whatever comes, at the same time doing my best to achieve my valid goals."

The secret of overcoming irritation is to view life in terms of its longer rhythms: not the fleeting ripples of pleasure and pain, but the broad waves of long-term loyalties; and not emotional commitments merely, but the great swells of dedication to high aims in life.

DAY TWENTY-TWO

The secret of overcoming negativity is to understand that what you behold in the world reflects back to you what you are in yourself. Work at self-transformation. Stop thinking that the world owes it to you to grant your every wish!

D A Y T W E N T Y - T H R E E

The secret of overcoming insecurity is to visualize yourself as seated at the heart of infinity. For the universe, as far as your own awareness is concerned, is centered in yourself. Send forth rays of faith and good will to all, and life will sustain you in every difficulty.

DAY TWENTY-FOUR

The secret of overcoming jealousy is to realize that no human being ever owns another; each stands alone before eternity. That man or woman most truly loves who is inwardly free, and who grants perfect freedom to all. Everyone must grow at his own pace, to find his rightful position in the great scheme of things.

DAY TWENTY-FIVE

The secret of overcoming conceit is to view the universe as center everywhere, circumference nowhere. Each human being lives at the heart of a vast reality. Remember, the need of everyone to seek his own approach to truth is quite as important as your own. Above all, see God's presence at that universal center as the true causative factor.

DAY TWENTY-SIX

The secret of overcoming resentment is to affirm, "I am free in myself!" — and to wish the same freedom for all. Radiate kindness outward from your heart. Be a source of happiness to others if you, too, would know happiness.

*The secret of overcoming self-pity is to recognize that this kind of self-indulgence only limits your ability to overcome your difficulties. Become a conqueror! Remember, whatever any human being has ever achieved, **you** can achieve! All that is necessary is patience, sensitive insight, and determination. Every seeming limitation is in fact an opportunity for shining victory!*

DAY TWENTY-EIGHT

The secret of overcoming low self-esteem is to realize that you are an integral part of everything that is — sustained forever by that Power which brought the very universe into existence. Open your heart to life! Cease seeing yourself as a lonely plant, waterless on an empty desert!

The secret of overcoming fear of failure is not to be attached to success. Concentrate on will power and energy, which bring success. Even your failures, then, will become steppingstones to ever-greater achievements.

DAY THIRTY

The secret of overcoming fear of death is to deepen your awareness of that central part in your being which never changes, but weaves like a thread through life's tapestry of apparently unrelated circumstances. The consciousness of change is allied to the fear of death. But to see changelessness at the heart of change is the secret of immortality.

DAY THIRTY-ONE

Other Books in the Secrets Series by J. Donald Walters

Secrets of Love
Secrets of Friendship
Secrets of Happiness
Secrets for Men
Secrets for Women
Secrets of Success
Secrets of Prosperity
Secrets of Leadership

Secrets of Winning People
Secrets of Inner Peace
Secrets of Self-Acceptance
Secrets of Radiant Health and Well-Being

(for children)
Life's Little Secrets
Little Secrets of Success
Little Secrets of Happiness
Little Secrets of Friendship

Selected Other Titles by J. Donald Walters

Expansive Marriage

Money Magnetism

Education for Life

The Artist as a Channel

The Art of Supportive Leadership

Affirmations for Self-Healing

[illegible]

[illegible]

[illegible]

[illegible]